# The Way to the Orsay Museum

Written by Hyo-mi Park
Illustrated by Jae-seon Ahn
Edited by Joy Cowley

big & SMALL

Marie was very excited.
She was going with her mother
to see the painting *Water Lilies*
at the Orsay Museum.
Her mother said, "We must hurry.
There will be a long line
at the museum."

Mom didn't need to worry.
Marie was ready to go.

Mom said, "That's the Pompidou Centre.
Shall we stop there for a visit?"

Marie shook her head. Her school had visited
the house and garden of the artist Claude Monet.
Marie had seen beautiful water lilies there,
and her teacher had told her that Monet
had painted them. Now she wanted to see
his painting *Water Lillies* in the Orsay Museum.

"No thanks. We are going to see *Water Lilies*.
Let's hurry, Mom. The line will be long."

Monet's house is in the village of Giverny
in north-west France. Here visitors can
see the home and art studio of Monet
who was an Impressionist painter, and
the garden that inspired much of his work.

5

They went by the River Seine,
where many people walked their dogs.
Marie missed her dog, Antis,
and wished she had brought him.
Then she remembered that dogs
cannot go into museums.

Ahead of them was the Louvre Museum.
There were many artworks in there.
"Do you want to go to the Louvre instead?"
asked Marie's mother.

"No. I want to see *Water Lilies*!" said Marie.

They walked over a bridge.
There were sculptures here and there.
Mom looked at each sculpture
and stopped in front of a large cat.
Marie purred like a cat and said,
"*Meow?* Mom? Let's hurry up
or we'll be last in the line."

At the end of the bridge,
a man was playing the violin
and an artist was drawing
the violinist. Both men had
rapidly moving hands
that were interesting to watch.

"Mom, we should go now," said Marie.

"There's the Orsay Museum," said Mom.

"My teacher told us that it used to be
a train station long ago," said Marie.
"Come on. We need to get in line."

They were in front of the museum,
standing in a long, long line.
"We should have come earlier!"
Marie complained to her mother.

"But there was so much to see
on the way to the museum,"
replied her mother.

"My legs are getting tired,"
Marie grumbled.

At last they were in the museum.
Mom wanted to look at the sculptures.
There were so many amazing pieces of art.
Marie grabbed Mom's hand and pulled.
*"Water Lilies! Water Lilies!"* she said.

19

In the exhibition hall, Mom stopped
in front of a beautiful painting
of a farmer and his wife praying.
Marie stopped, too.

They both looked for a long time
and Marie said, "I've seen this
painting in a book at school."

Finally they arrived at the *Water Lilies* painting. Marie remembered the water lilies she had seen in Monet's garden. These lilies looked different. They were kind of smudgy.

"Marie, paintings are not photographs," explained Mom. "The artist wants you to feel something about his painting. He wants you to get a feeling about the way he sees water lilies."

Marie stared at the painting for a long time.

Now Marie was really tired
and her legs were sore.

"Why don't we see more paintings?"
her mother asked her.

"We can come back another time,"
said Marie. "Now I'm hungry.
Let's go and have some lunch."

## About France

# A Country of Culture and Art

The blue part of the French flag represents freedom, and the white stands for equality. The red means love for all people. These were the colors of the citizens' hats during the French Revolution when they fought against their rulers for freedom and equality.

## Paris, the Capital City Loved by Artists

France is located in the center of Western Europe. Many important roads pass through Paris, the capital of France, a city that has always been focused on the arts. Marie and her mother saw the works of many artists on their way to the Orsay Museum.

Eiffel Tower, the symbol of Paris.

Art of the 20th century is exhibited at the Pompidou Centre.

## Pompidou Centre

The Pompidou Centre is a complex built in Paris in 1977. At first glance, it looks like a factory because the pipes and steel structure are on the outside of the building. It was built to capture a "culture of factory" atmosphere. It contains a theater, a center for music and acoustic research, and the French National Museum of Modern Art.

## The World-renowned Louvre Museum

The Louvre Museum was once a palace, but after the French Revolution, it became a museum. It is one of the world's greatest art museums, housing approximately 400,000 artworks, from ancient art through to Renaissance painting and Classical art. Da Vinci's famous painting the *Mona Lisa* is in the Louvre.

The glass pyramid is the entrance to the Louvre Museum.

## Orsay Museum Was a Train Station

The building that houses the Orsay Museum was a train station for 40 years from 1900. After the station closed, it reopened as a museum in 1986. From then on, 19th-century artworks from the Louvre were moved here. It contains many famous works of the Impressionist painters, such as Manet, Monet, Degas, and Renoir.

The Orsay Museum by the River Seine

Monet studied the relation between light and subject, and how that changed depending on the time of day.

## Monet, Painter of Light

Claude Monet was a famous French artist who was fascinated by the way scenes changed with the light. As Monet grew older, he painted in his house at Giverny. He often painted the lily pond in front of his house, and his water lily paintings are exhibited in a number of museums worldwide.

## Fertile Land

Three sides of hexagonal-shaped France have coastlines. These face the English Channel, the Atlantic Ocean, and the Mediterranean Sea. The climate varies, depending on the distance from the coast, so various wines grow in different areas. High quality grains and meat are produced on the spacious fertile plains, and seafood is obtained from the ocean. The cuisine in France is highly developed and considered to be the best in the world.

Saint- Émilion is a key wine town in the Libournais district of Bordeaux.

## Food for Royalty Became Food for Everyone!

Once, the royal family and nobles hired chefs to create delicious food. After the French Revolution, the chefs could no longer work at the palace, so they opened high quality restaurants. That is how fine dining was introduced to the citizens of France and the world generally. Wine is usually served with French food and used in cooking, so French people store wine in their homes.

Snails, a French gourmet dish.

# A Conversation with Etienne, Who Lives in France

### Please introduce yourself.

My name is Etienne Deroubaise. I am ten years old and I live in Paris, France. My family includes my parents and my older brothers, Eliott and Alex.

### Have you been to a museum?

Yes, I've been to the Orsay Museum, the Louvre Museum, the Picasso Museum and the Pompidou Centre. My favorite is the Louvre, and my favorite artist is Pablo Picasso.

### What do you like about Picasso?

Picasso's paintings are interesting and unique. His techniques are different from other artists.

### Which of Picasso's works do you like?

I like his portrait paintings. The faces and expressions are funny.

### Do you have a wish, Etienne?

I like travelling so much! I've been to Tunisia, Crete in Greece, and Sicily. I wish I had the power to fly so I could travel to more places whenever I want to.

United Kingdom

Calais

English Channel

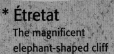

* **Étretat**
The magnificent elephant-shaped cliff

● Brest

* **Savate**
France's traditional martial art, similar to kickboxing

Atlantic Ocean

# France

Name: Republic of France

Location: Western Europe

Area: 211,208 mi² (547,030 km²)

Capital: Paris

Population: Approx. 65.7 million (2012)

Language: French

Main religion: Catholicism (Christianity)

Main exports: Agricultural products, chemical products, machinery, electrical products, cars, wine

* **Foie Gras**
A French food made from the liver of a duck or goose

Bordeaux

* **Wine**
An alcoholic drink commonly served with meals in France

Spain

* **Escargot**
A variety of edible snails, common on menus in France

Belgium

Luxembourg

Germany

* Eiffel Tower
The famous iron
lattice tower in Paris

Paris

Versailles

* TGV
France's high-speed railway
service, travels at a speed
of 200 miles per hour

Switzerland

* Perfume
France is world-famous for
the perfumes it makes

Italy

Lyon

*France

* Chamonix Mont-Blanc
Resort city where the snow-covered
Mont-Blanc can be seen all year round

Nice

* Can-Can
A lively, high-kicking
stage dance

Mediterranean Sea

Corsica

Original Korean text by Hyo-mi Park

Illustrations by Jae-seon Ahn

Korean edition © Aram Publishing

This English edition published by big & SMALL in 2016
by arrangement with Aram Publishing

English text edited by Joy Cowley

English edition © big & SMALL 2016

ISBN: 978-1-925247-24-4

Printed in Korea